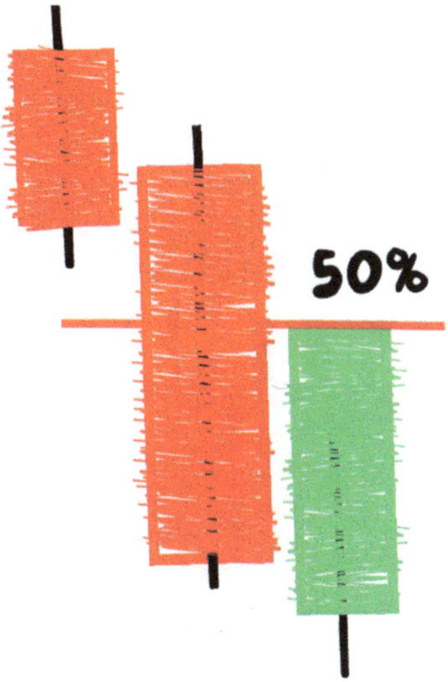
50%

JULYTHIRTY co.

by Chaymeriyia Moncrief

DISCLAIMER

The information provided in Little Black Book of Candlestick Patterns is for educational and informational purposes only. This book is not intended to provide financial, investment, or trading advice. Trading stocks, options, forex, and other financial instruments involves significant risk, and past performance of any strategy or pattern does not guarantee future results.

The author and publisher are not registered financial advisors, brokers, or investment professionals. Readers should conduct their own research, consult with a qualified financial professional, and fully understand the risks before making any trading or investment decisions. The strategies and patterns discussed in this book are tools to assist traders in market analysis but should not be relied upon as sole decision-making criteria.

The author and publisher are not responsible for any financial losses or damages resulting from the use of the information in this book. By reading this book, you acknowledge and accept that all trading and investment decisions are made at your own risk.

BOOK USAGE

The candlestick patterns in the Little Black Book of Candlestick Patterns are universal tools used by traders across all financial markets, including stocks, forex, cryptocurrencies, commodities, and futures. Their application is not exclusive to any single market or strategy; for decades, these formations have been recognized and utilized by traders and analysts worldwide.

While a pattern's effectiveness can vary with market conditions, timeframes, and individual trading styles, the underlying principles remain consistent across all financial instruments. This book is a guide to identifying and understanding these patterns, but successful trading also requires careful risk management, an awareness of market context, and personal experience. Therefore, readers should use these patterns as one component of a broader strategy and always conduct their own due diligence before making any trade.

THE BOOK'S CONTENTS

SINGLE CANDLES PG. 12

DOUBLE CANDLES PG. 26

TRIPLE CANDLES PG. 36

CANDLE FORMS PG. 47

GAPS PG. 65

QUIZ

QUIZ PG. 71

"A CANDLE LOSES NOTHING BY LIGHTING ANOTHER CANDLE, BUT IN TRADING, EVERY CANDLE TELLS A STORY OF BUYERS AND SELLERS FIGHTING FOR CONTROL."

– UNKNOWN

THERE ARE STORIES IN THOSE CANDLES

INTRO

Staring at a stock chart and wondering what on earth those little red and green candles are trying to say? Yep, been there. If you're nodding along, then congrats you're about to crack the code. This guide was made for beginners who want to figure out why prices move, catch the next big wave, and trade smarter.

How? By using a super cool, old-school tool called candlestick patterns. They might look like weird little blobs, but each one is a snapshot of what traders are feeling: the good (greed!), the bad (fear!), and the ugly (panic!) all rolled into a single candle.

WHY THIS BOOK?

Trading can feel overwhelming, especially when you're bombarded with indicators, complex strategies, and fancy explanations. But here's the thing—before algorithms and indicators, traders relied on pure candles & price action to make decisions.

- 50 powerful candlestick patterns that can help you predict price movements.
- Easy-to-understand explanations; no boring textbook definitions here.
- How to use these patterns in real-world trading—because theory is useless without application.

WHO IT'S FOR?

- Day traders, swing traders, and scalpers who rely on quick market moves.
- Beginners who want to learn the foundation of technical analysis.
  Experienced traders looking to sharpen their pattern recognition skills.
- Anyone who's tired of guessing when to buy and sell.

Each candlestick pattern in this book is broken down without the confusing financial mumbo jumbo; just clear, practical insights that help you spot opportunities and avoid bad trades. By the end of this book, you'll not only recognize these patterns but also understand when they actually matter and how to use them to your advantage.

UNIT ONE

CANDLESTICK PATTERNS

CANDLE ANATOMY

The thick part in the middle of the candle? That's the body where price actually spent most of its time during that period. If the body is green (or white, depending on the chart colors), it means price closed higher than it opened; buyers were in control. If the body is red (or black), price closed lower than it opened, sellers won that round. Big body = Strong momentum (big fight, but one side clearly won). Small body = Weak momentum (buyers and sellers were kind of evenly matched).

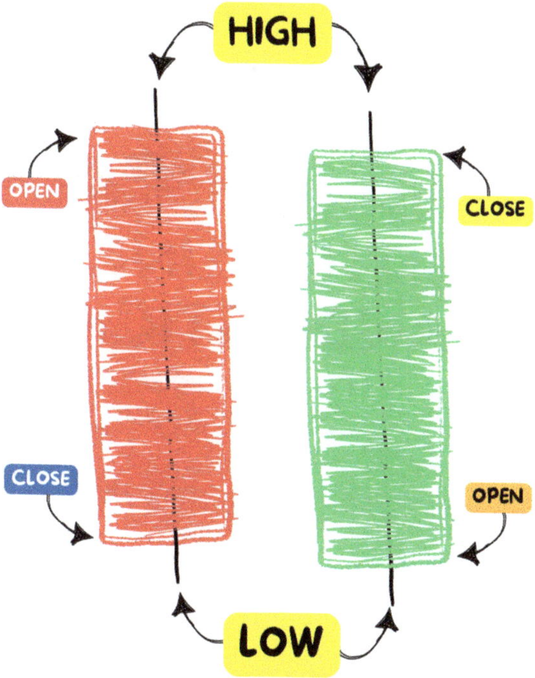

CANDLE

SINGLES

IDENTIFY SINGLE CANDLESTICKS

DOJI

A Doji looks like a tiny cross because the opening and closing prices are the same (or very close). It means the market couldn't decide whether to go up or down. Buyers and sellers kept battling, but in the end, nobody won. If you see this after a strong trend, it might be a warning sign that the trend is running out of steam.

DRAGONFLY DOJI

Imagine prices crashing down early in the day, but suddenly, buyers step in and push them right back up to where they started. That's the Dragonfly Doji. It looks like a "T" and signals that buyers have some fight left. If this appears after a downtrend, it could be a sign that the bulls (buyers) are about to take over.

GRAVESTONE DOJI

Opposite of the Dragonfly, the Gravestone Doji looks like an upside-down "T." The price started low, shot up during the session, but then collapsed back down to where it started. This tells us that sellers won the battle and could signal an upcoming downtrend.

HAMMER

This candlestick literally looks like a hammer. The price dropped but then rebounded strongly to close near the opening price. It means that buyers stepped in hard after an sell-off. If you see this after a downtrend, it's a bullish sign that the trend could reverse.

INVERTED HAMMER

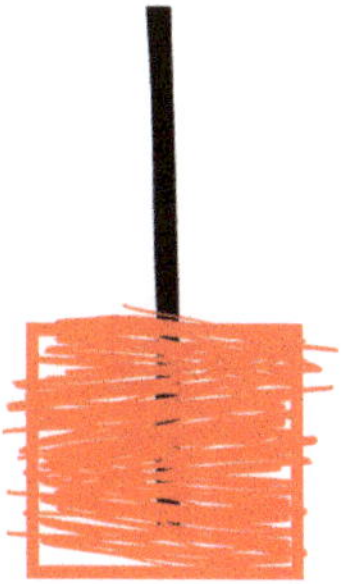

The Inverted Hammer looks like a flipped version of the Hammer. The price tried to go up, but sellers knocked it back down. However, if this happens after a downtrend, it still means buyers are waking up. You'll need confirmation (another bullish candle after it to trust the reversal.

HANGING MAN

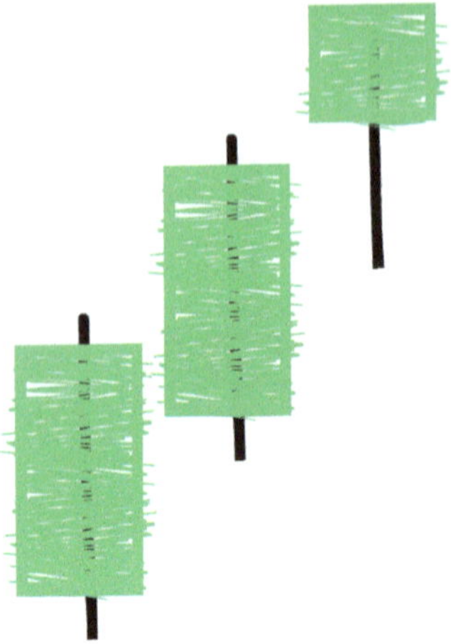

The Hanging Man is just a Hammer but found at the top of an uptrend. It means the price went lower during the day, but buyers pushed it back up. However, since it appears after a rally, it's actually a warning sign that the trend might be tapping out.

SPINNING TOP

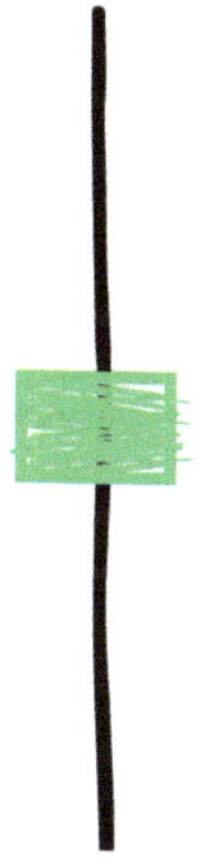

A Spinning Top looks like a small candle with long wicks on both sides. This tells you that both buyers and sellers tried to push the price in different directions, but in the end, it didn't go anywhere. It's a sign of market hesitation, meaning traders aren't sure what to do next. Wait for confirmation.

LONG LEG DOJI

This candlestick screams indecision. It has super long wicks on both sides and a tiny or nonexistent body. It means the market went on a wild ride up and down, but ultimately, it closed right around where it opened.

BEARISH PIN BARS

A bearish pin bar is a candlestick that shows price is likely to go down. It has a small body and a long wick (shadow) sticking up.

When you see a bearish pin bar, it's showing that buyers tried to push the price up, but sellers took over and pushed it back down before the candle closed. That's why the long wick is on top and the small body is near the bottom of the candle.

BULLISH PIN BARS

A bullish pin bar is the opposite of a bearish one. It shows that price is likely to go up.

A bullish pin bar has a small body at the top and a long wick (shadow) sticking down. This means that during that candle, sellers tried to push the price down, but buyers came in strong and pushed it back up before the candle closed.

MARUBOZU

BULLISH

A Bullish Marubozu is a solid green candle with no wicks. That means the price opened at its lowest and closed at its highest. It's like a power move by buyers; they dominated the market all day. This will provide different insights on different timeframes. Expect more upside momentum!

MARUBOZU

BEARISH

A Bearish Marubozu is the exact opposite; a big red candle with no wicks. That means the price opened at its highest and closed at its lowest. Sellers controlled the entire session, and this could mean more downside ahead.

4 PRICE DOJI

INDICATES ZERO VOLUME

A Four Price Doji is one of the rarest candlestick patterns you'll see on a chart. It happens when the open, high, low, and close prices are all exactly the same. This means the price didn't really move at all during the given time period. The candle itself looks like a simple horizontal line with no upper or lower wick because there was no difference between the highest and lowest price.

CANDLE DOUBLES

IDENTIFY DUO CANDLESTICKS

BULLISH ENGULFING

A Bullish Engulfing is a strong reversal signal. It happens when a small red candle (indicating selling pressure) is followed by a big green candle (indicating buying pressure). The green candle completely engulfs the red one, showing that the buyers have overpowered the sellers.

BEARISH ENGULFING

The Bearish Engulfing is basically the opposite of the Bullish Engulfing. It happens when a small green candle is followed by a big red candle. This big red candle completely engulfs the previous green one, signaling that the bulls have lost control and the bears have taken over.

TWEEZER BOTTOM

AWAIT FOR CONFIRMATION ON THE 2ND OR 3RD CANDLE DEPENDING ON YOUR TIMEFRAME.

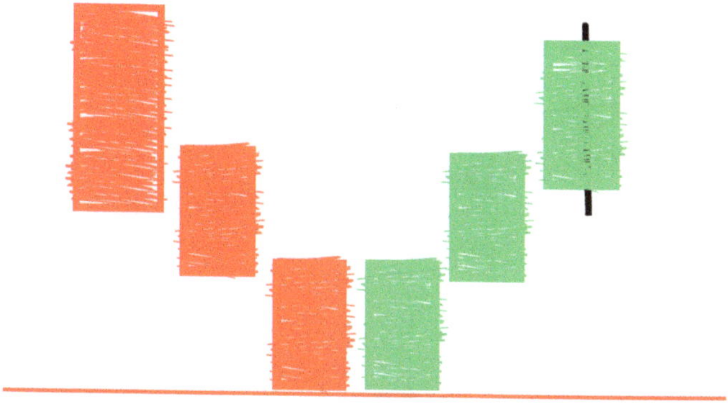

A Tweezer Bottom happens <u>when you get two candles that have equal lows.</u> The first one might be a red candle (showing the market has been going down), but then the second candle, even if it's green, also touches the same low. This shows that buying pressure is stepping in at the same price level.

TWEEZER TOP

AWAIT FOR CONFIRMATION ON THE 2ND OR 3RD CANDLE DEPENDING ON YOUR TIMEFRAME.

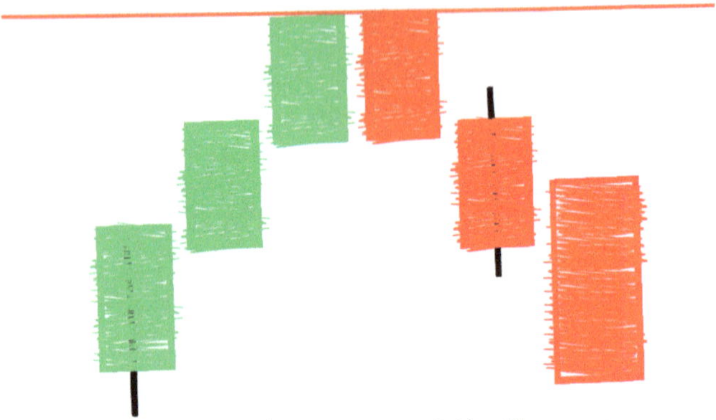

A Tweezer Top is the opposite of the Tweezer Bottom. It happens when you have two candles with equal highs. The first candle could be green (indicating the market has been going up), but the second candle reaches the same high but ends as a red candle. This shows that sellers are coming in at the same price level and the bulls' momentum is fading.

INSIDE BAR

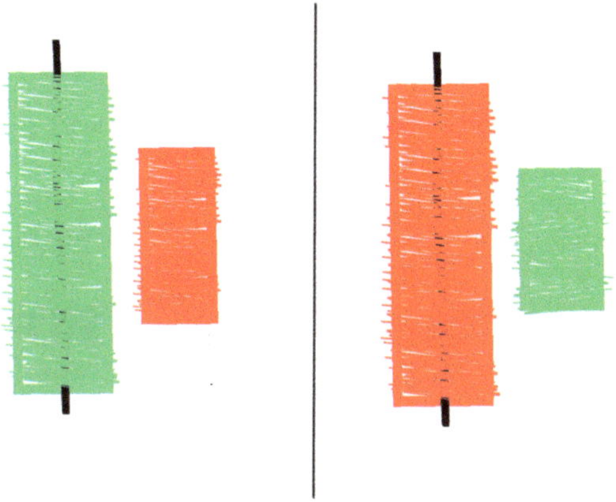

An inside bar is like a moment of hesitation in the market. Picture a big candle, and then right after it, a smaller candle that stays completely within the range of the previous one. It's like price is pausing, catching its breath before making its next move. This pattern usually signals that a breakout is coming; whether up or down depends on the trend and other factors. If it breaks above the high of the first candle, it's a bullish sign. If it breaks below, it could be bearish.

PIERCING PATTERN

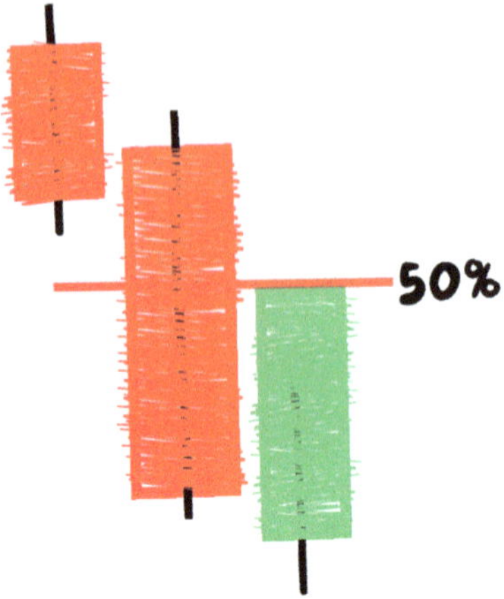

A piercing pattern is a red candle followed by a green candle that opens below the low of the red candle but closes halfway or more into the body of the red candle. The bulls are reversing the downward movement by pushing the price up. It's a bullish sign, indicating a potential uptrend.

HARAMI

BULLISH

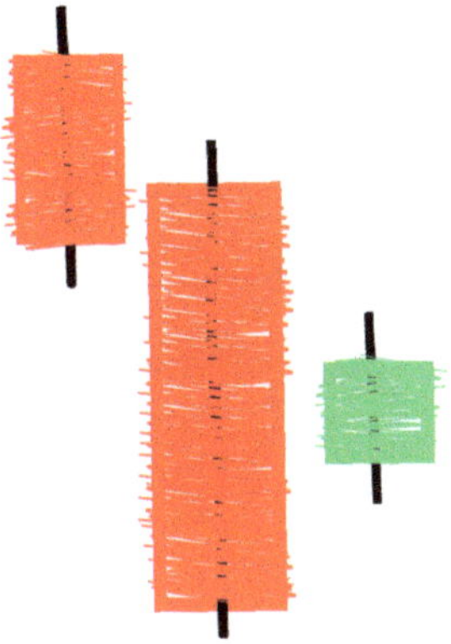

A Harami (Bullish) pattern is a bullish reversal that happens when a big red candle is followed by a small green candle that is completely inside the red candle's body. The green candle's body is contained within the previous red candle, and this shows that selling pressure is fading.

HARAMI

BEARISH

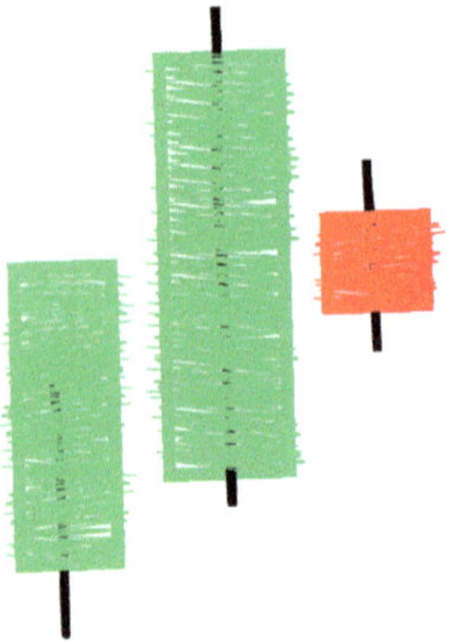

The Harami (Bearish) pattern is the opposite of the bullish version. It happens when a big green candle is followed by a small red candle, with the red candle completely inside the green candle's body.

SHOOTING STAR

The Shooting Star is like a market head fake—it looks like pric- es are going up, but then they get smacked right back down. This pattern forms when the price shoots up during a session but then gets rejected hard, leaving behind a small body and a long upper wick.

CANDLE

TRIPLES

IDENTIFY TRIO
CANDLESTICKS

UPSIDE TASUKI GAP

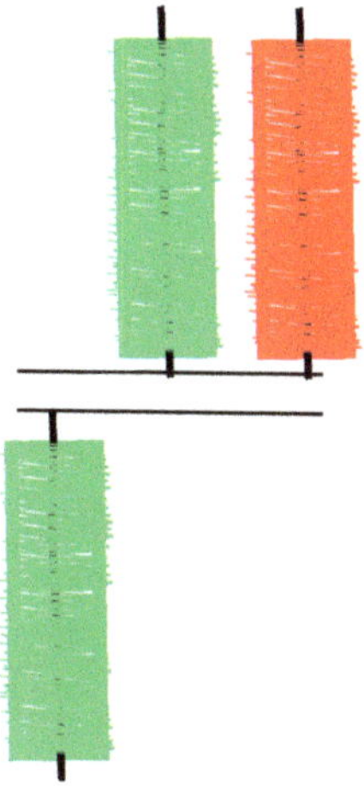

The Upside Tasuki Gap is a bullish continuation pattern that appears during an uptrend, signaling that the trend is likely to resume after a brief pause. It is formed by three candles: first, a strong green candle, followed by a second green candle that gaps up, indicating strong buying momentum. The third candle is a red candle that opens within the body of the second and closes down inside the gap, but crucially, does not fill it.

DOWNSIDE TASUKI GAP

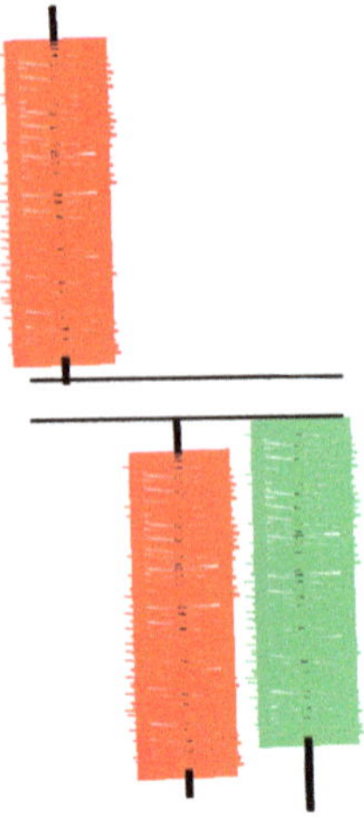

The Downside Tasuki Gap is a three-candle bearish continuation pattern that occurs during a downtrend. It begins with two red candles, where the second candle gaps down from the first, signifying intense selling pressure. This is followed by a green candle that attempts to rally but fails to completely close the gap. This failure by the buyers to reclaim the gapped-down price level demonstrates their weakness and indicates that the brief pause is over.

MORNING STAR

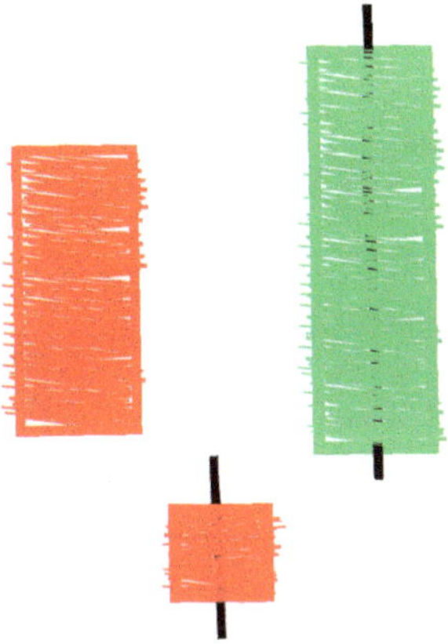

The Morning Star is like a "wake-up call" for the market when it's been sleeping in a downtrend. You get a red candle (the market is clearly going down), followed by a small indecisive candle (this could be a Doji or a small body candle showing that neither the bulls nor the bears are in control), and then a big green candle (the bulls are coming in strong, reversing the trend).

MORNING DOJI STAR

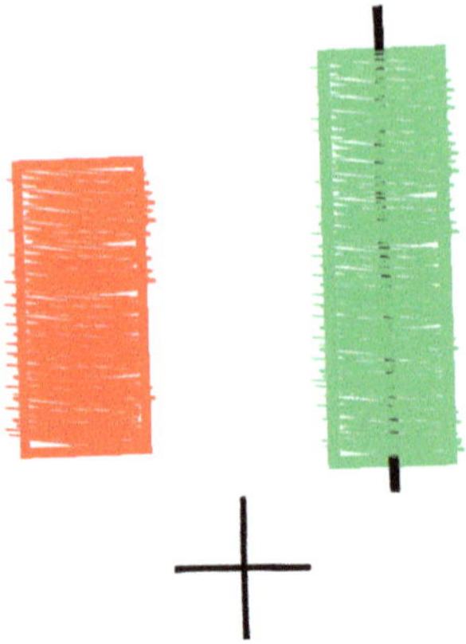

A variation of the Morning Star where the middle candle (at the bottom of the move) is a Doji, signifying strong indecision before the reversal.

EVENING STAR

The Evening Star is basically the opposite of the Morning Star. It's like a "watch out!" warning when the market's been climbing. The first candle is a green candle (the market's been going up), followed by a small indecisive candle (again, this could be a Doji, indicating indecision), and then a big red candle (the bears take over).

EVENING DOJI STAR

A variation of the Evening Star where the middle candle (at the top of the move) is a Doji, signifying strong indecision before the reversal.

THREE WHITE SOLIDERS

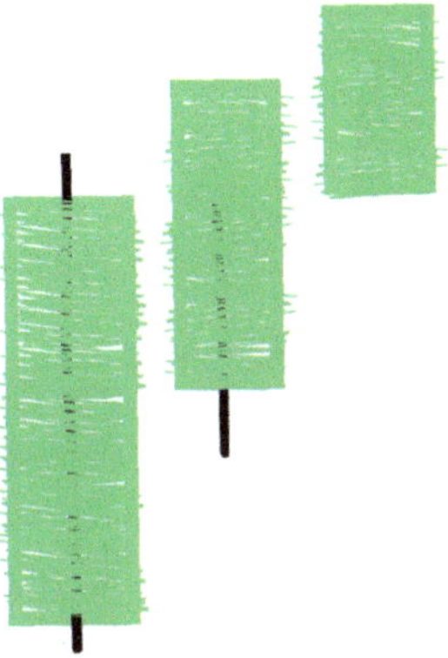

The Three White Soldiers pattern is a solid confirmation that the market is in an uptrend. You'll see three strong green candles in a row, each opening above the previous candle's close and closing higher each time. The price moves up steadily, without much retracement.

It's a classic bullish continuation pattern; a signal that the uptrend is still going strong. Think of it as the market saying, "We're not done moving up yet!" The candles are long, green, and steady, showing that the bulls have been in control for an extended period.

THREE BLACK CROWS

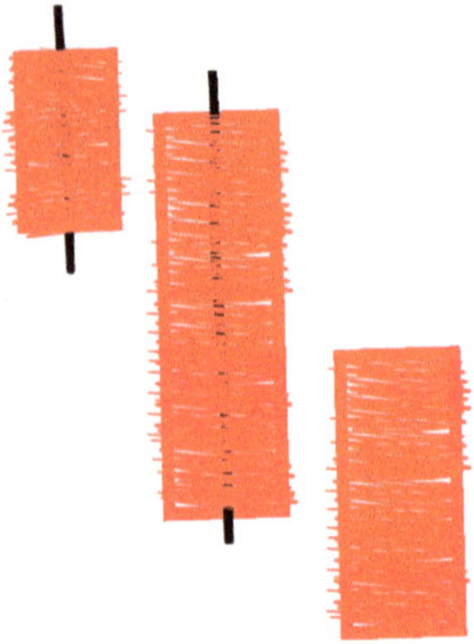

The Three Black Crows is the opposite of the Three White Soldiers. This pattern consists of three strong red candles in a row, each opening below the previous candle's close and closing lower each time. It's like a steady decline, with each candle showing increasing selling pressure.

This is a *bearish continuation pattern*, signaling that the downtrend is strong and likely to continue.

RISING THREE

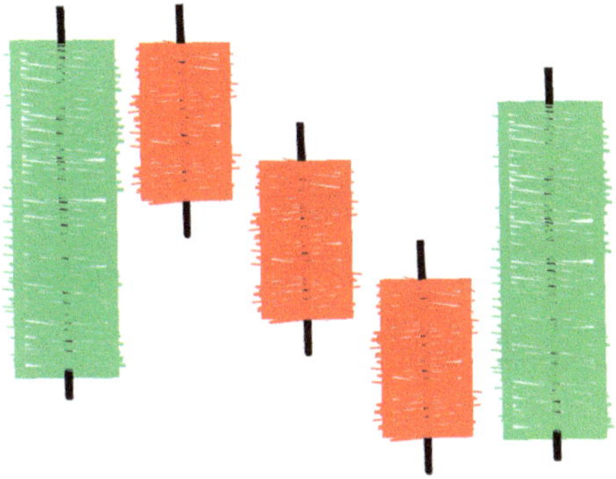

This pattern is like a pit stop in a strong uptrend before the price continues to climb. You start with a big green candle (buyers are in control), followed by three small red candles (looks like a slight pullback, but nothing major), and then a big green candle again (buyers are back in charge and pushing the price higher).

FALLING THREE

This is just the opposite of the Rising Three Methods. You start with a big red candle (sellers in control), followed by three small green candles (a tiny push-up, but nothing strong), and then another big red candle (sellers take over again and drive the price lower).

The market pauses but doesn't reverse. Those three small green candles might seem like buyers are trying to push the price up, but they're weak.

CANDLE

FORMS

IDENTIFY FULL FORMATIONS

BULL FLAG-A

CONSOLIDATION CAN GO ON FOR AN EXTENDED PERIOD OF TIME.

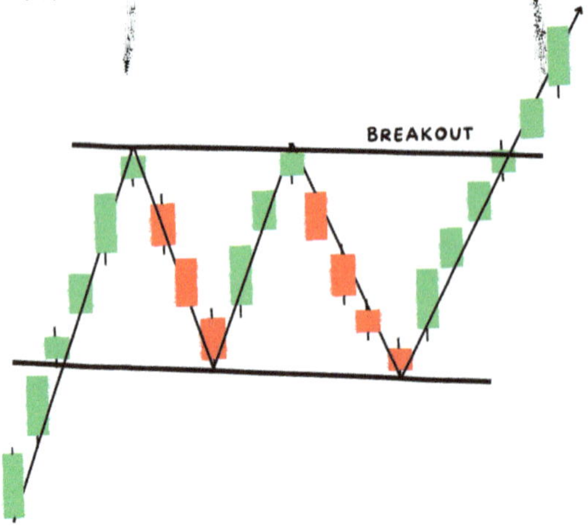

Imagine the market is sprinting upward, and then it needs a quick break before running again. That's exactly what a Bullish Flag is! You'll see a strong upward move, followed by a small, downward-sloping or sideways consolidation (it literally looks like a flag), and then, boom! Another breakout to the upside.

BULL FLAG-B

BULL FLAGS CAN ALSO CONSOLIDATE DOWNWARD.

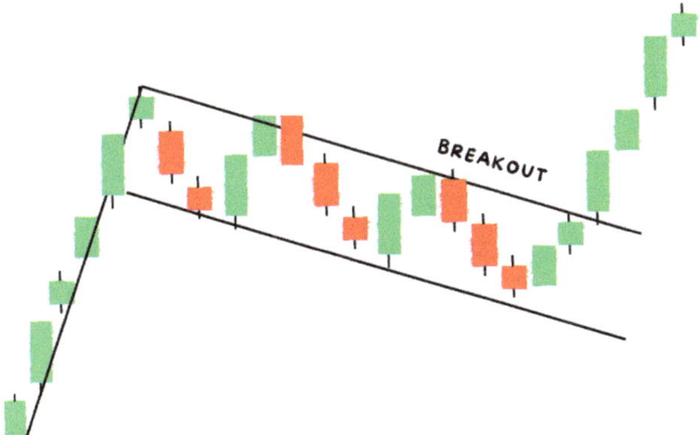

BEAR FLAG-A

CONSOLIDATION CAN GO ON FOR AN EXTENDED PERIOD OF TIME.

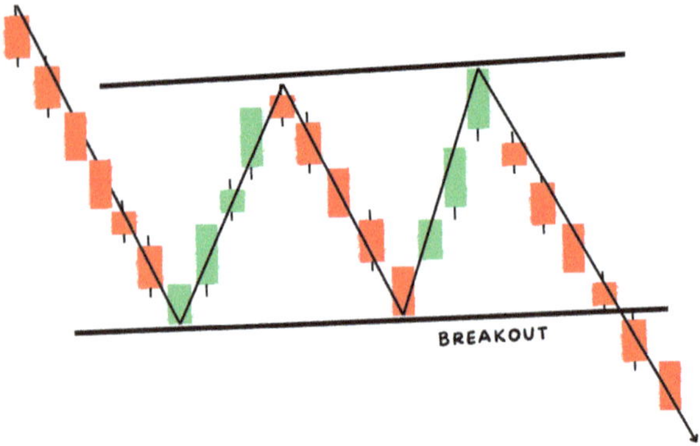

Now flip that Bullish Flag upside down, and you've got a Bearish Flag. The market dumps hard, then pauses in a small upward-sloping or sideways pattern, and then it breaks down again.

The price is just resting before another drop. The small up- ward consolidation might look like buyers are stepping in, but really, it's just a weak bounce before the market continues falling.

MINI-TASK

BEAR FLAG-B

DRAW A OUTLINE OR CANDLES TO FORM A SECONDARY BEAR FLAG.

BEAR PENNANT

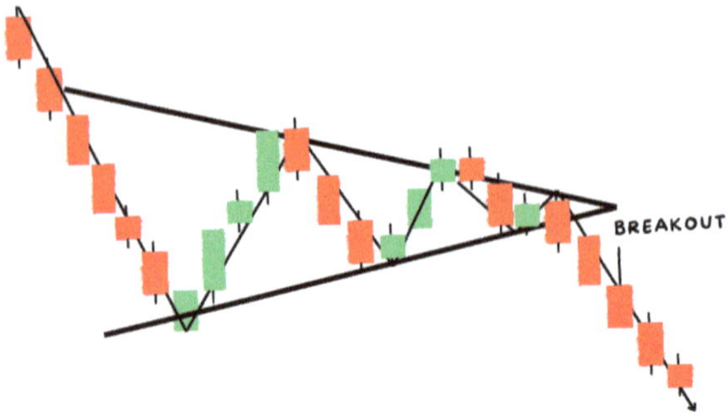

A *bear pennant* forms when the price falls hard ; that's called the flagpole. After that, instead of just falling straight down, it starts moving sideways into a small, tight triangle shape. This little triangle is the pennant.

Once that triangle is done forming, the price usually breaks out at the *bottom* and continues falling. So, in simple words, it looks like a *big drop*, a small sideways triangle, and then another drop after.

BULL PENNANT

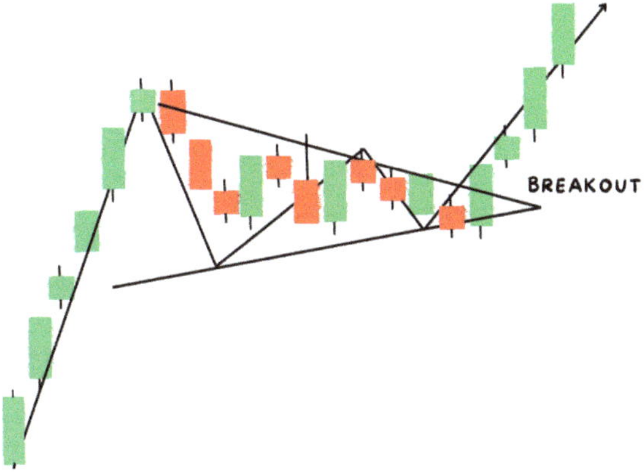

A bull pennant is the opposite of a bear pennant. It happens when the market is going up, then takes a quick break to consolidate. First, there's a big, sharp move up, called the flagpole. It then moves sideways into a small, tight triangle shape for a short time. This little triangle is the pennant.

DOUBLETOP

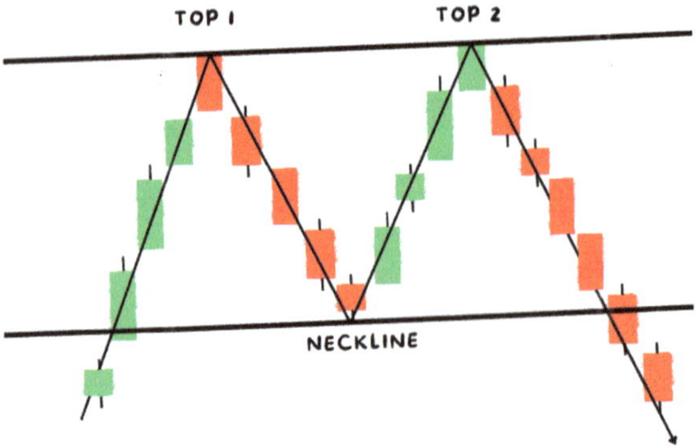

The double top is like price running up to a ceiling twice and failing both times. The first peak hits resistance, price pulls back, tries again, and fails at the same level. That second failure usually leads to a drop. It's a bearish reversal pattern because it shows buyers lost control, and sellers are taking over.

DOUBLEBOTTOM

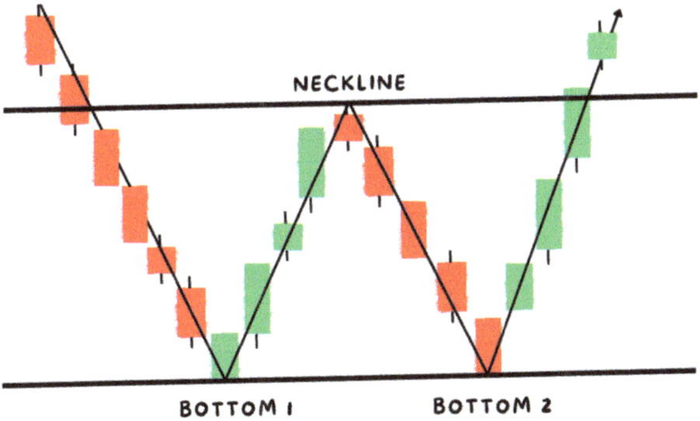

Flip the double top upside down, and you've got a double bottom. Price hits support, bounces up, comes back down to the same level, and bounces again. This tells you buyers are stepping in at that price level, preventing further drops. Once price breaks above the resistance between the two bottoms, it's a strong bullish signal.

TRIPLE TOP

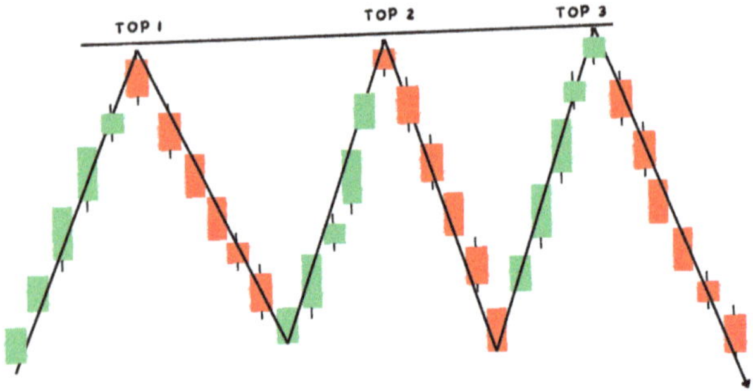

A Triple Top forms when the price moves up and <u>hits a strong resistance level three times but fails to break through.</u> It starts with an uptrend where buyers are in control, pushing the price higher. Eventually, the price reaches a level where sellers step in and push it back down. After this drop, buyers try again, bringing the price back up to the same level, only for it to be rejected once more. This happens a third time, and when the price fails to break resistance for the third time, it signals that buyers are losing strength.

TRIPLE BOTTOM

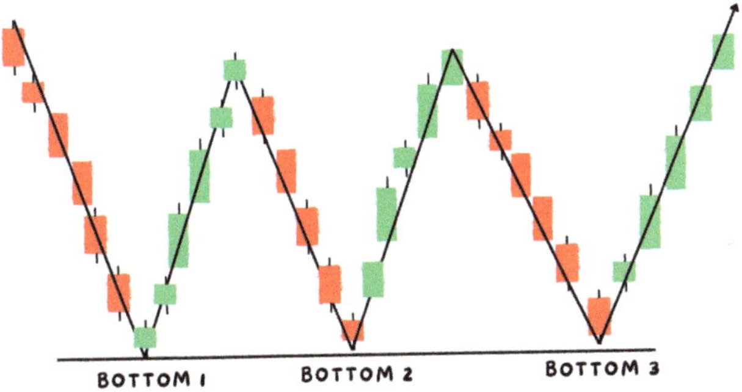

A Triple Bottom is the opposite of a Triple Top. It forms during a downtrend when the price falls and reaches a strong support level. Sellers push the price lower, but buyers step in and stop the decline. After bouncing off support, the price attempts to move high- er but struggles to maintain momentum, eventually falling back down to the same support level.

RISING WEDGE

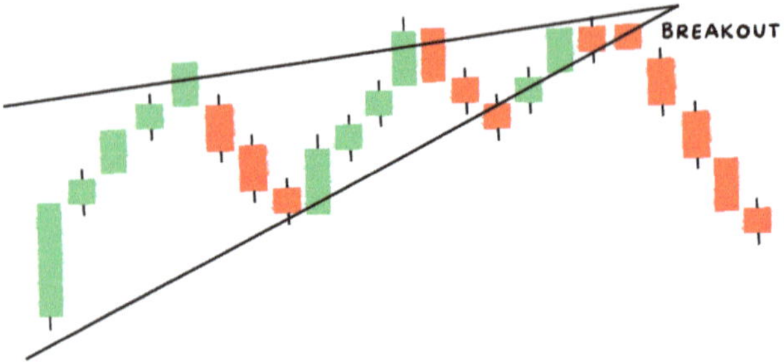

A rising wedge forms when the price is making higher highs and higher lows, but the trend lines that connect these points are converging. This means that while the market is still climbing, it's doing so with decreasing momentum. Eventually, the buyers start running out of steam, the candles get smaller and smaller and the price breaks downward. A rising wedge is generally considered a bearish pattern, and it usually appears after an uptrend, signaling that the market may be getting ready to reverse.

FALLING WEDGE

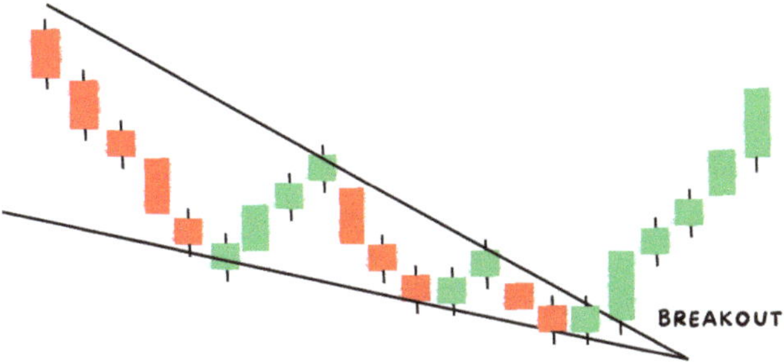

A falling wedge is the opposite. The price is making lower highs and lower lows, but just like in a rising wedge, the trend lines are getting closer together. This means sellers are in control, but they are losing momentum. Eventually, the pressure eases, and the price breaks upward. A falling wedge is a bullish pattern and often signals that a downtrend is about to reverse into an uptrend.

THE KEY THING ABOUT WEDGE PATTERNS IS THAT THEY INDICATE A SLOW DOWN IN MOMENTUM.

In a rising wedge, the buying pressure fades, leading to a breakdown. In a falling wedge, the selling pressure weakens, leading to a breakout. The breakout direction is crucial, and traders usually wait for confirmation before making a move, watching for a strong candle that breaks out of the wedge and holds.

Wedges can take time to form, and the longer they last, the bigger the breakout move tends to be. The volume also plays a role, volume decreases as the wedge tightens, and then a sudden spike in volume confirms the breakout. Whether it's a rising wedge pointing to a drop or a falling wedge hinting at a rally, these patterns are useful tools for spotting potential market moves before they happen.

CUP & HANDLE

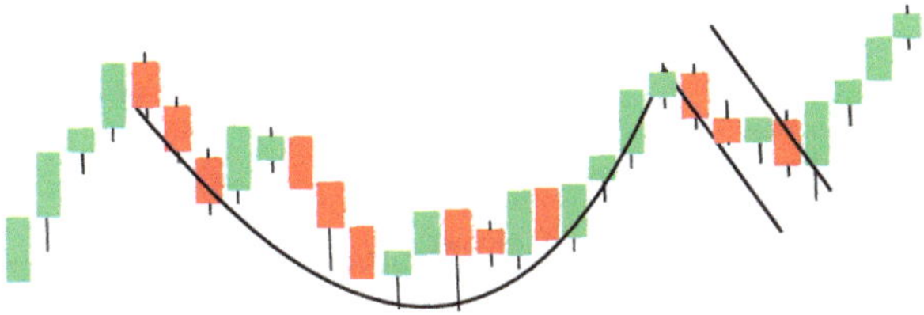

Imagine price forming a big U-shape, then pulling back slightly before pushing higher. That's the cup and handle pattern. The cup forms as price slowly rounds out, showing accumulation. Then comes a small dip (the handle), which is just the market shaking out weak hands before launching into a breakout.

HEAD & SHOULDERS

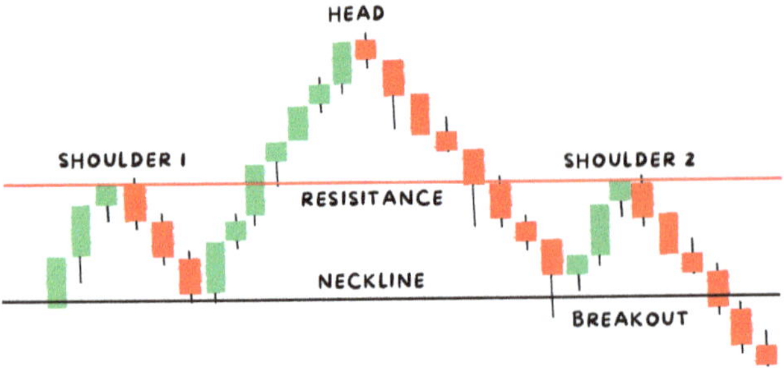

This one is a bearish reversal pattern that looks like, well, a head and shoulders. First, you get a peak (shoulder), then a higher peak (head), and finally another lower peak (shoulder). The key part is the "neckline," a support level connecting the lows. If price breaks below that, sellers take control, and the downtrend begins.

INVERTED HEAD & SHOULDERS

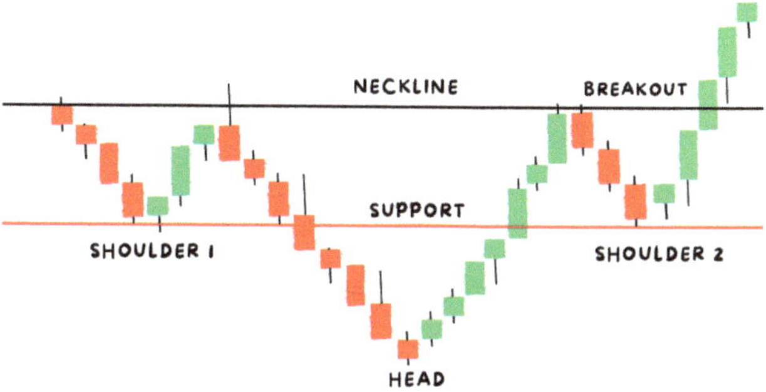

This is just the bullish version of the head and shoulders. Instead of peaks, you get three valleys. The middle one (head) dips the lowest, and the two shoulders form slightly higher lows at a support level. Once price breaks above the neckline, buyers take over, and an uptrend starts.

LADDER BOTTON

This is a complex but highly reliable five-candle bullish reversal pattern. Its name comes from the visual of the first four candles forming descending "rungs" down a ladder before the price action reverses. Finding a perfect Ladder Bottom is rare, but when it appears at the end of a prolonged downtrend, it signals a potential and often powerful trend reversal.

CHART

GAPS

IDENTIFY CANDLE CHART GAPS

ISLAND REVERSAL

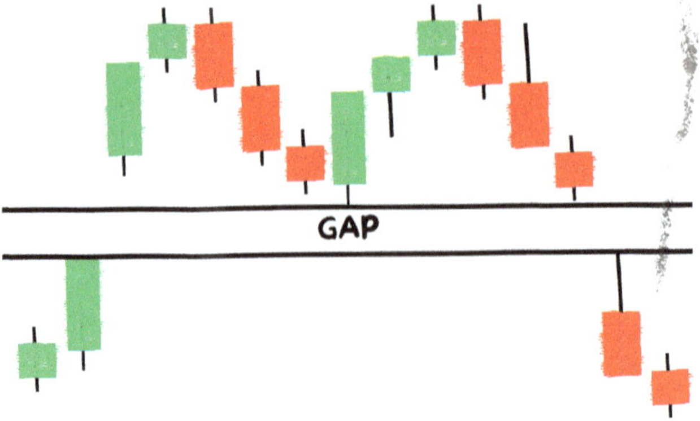

An island reversal is a pattern that shows a strong trend reversal is about to happen.

The price is goes up, then suddenly there's a gap up (price jumps higher and opens above the last candle). After trading there for a while (a few candles or days), the price suddenly gaps down (opens below the previous candle) and continues falling. That group of candles in the middle looks like it's stuck alone or "on an island" because there's a gap on both sides.

THE BREAK AWAY GAP

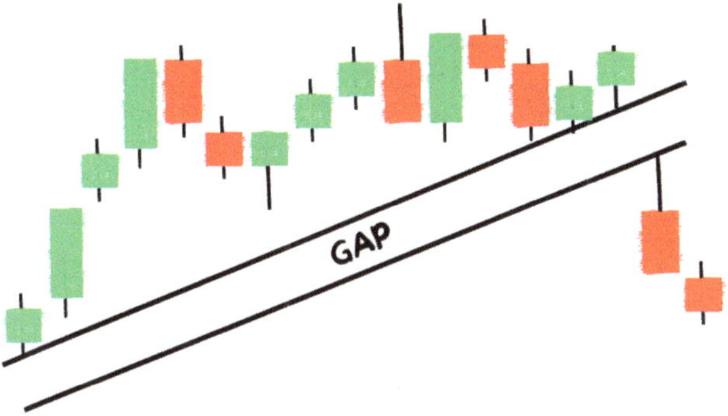

This is the market saying, "I'm outta here!" It happens when price gaps up or down at the start of a big move and just keeps going, leaving the previous range behind.

Usually happens after a period of consolidation or at key levels of support or resistance.

THE COMMON CHART GAP

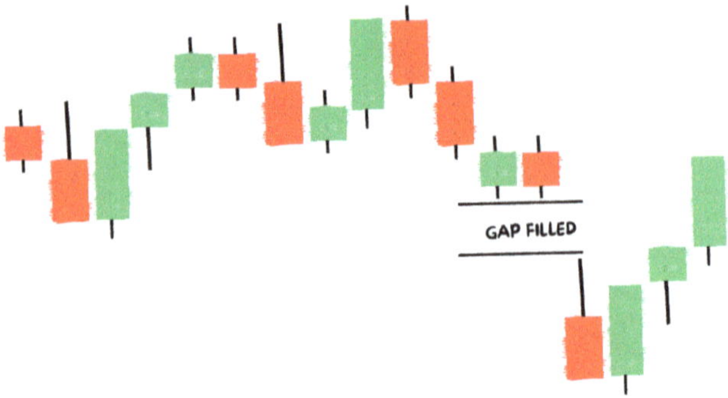

This is the most boring gap—just a small jump in price that usually gets filled pretty quickly.

Happens randomly, often in low-volume periods. No major trend shift or momentum behind it. Price usually comes back to fill the gap within a few sessions.

THE RUNAWAY CHART GAP

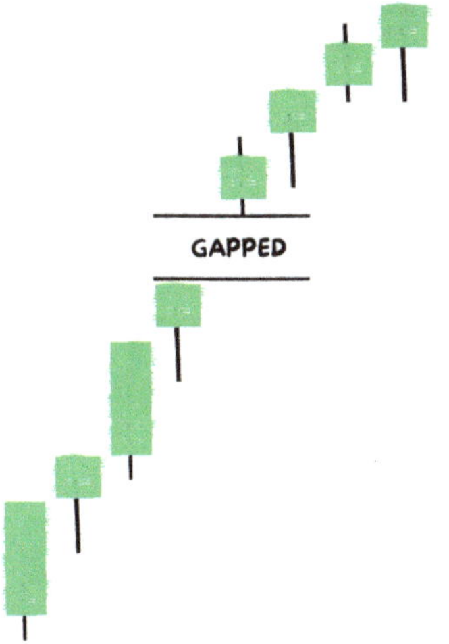

This gap appears in the middle of a strong trend, reinforcing that the move is nowhere near done. Happens when price is already moving strongly in one direction.

The market gaps and keeps going, like throwing more fuel on a fire. It's a sign that traders are jumping in, not taking profits; momentum is strong.

"LET THE MARKET TELL YOU WHAT TO DO. A CANDLESTICK PATTERN IS THE MARKET WHISPERING ITS NEXT MOVE."

– STEVE NISON (CREDITED WITH POPULARIZING CANDLESTICK CHARTS)

KNOWLEDGE

QUIZ

CAN YOU REMEMBER?

CANDLE KNOWLEDGE

NAME THE CANDLES

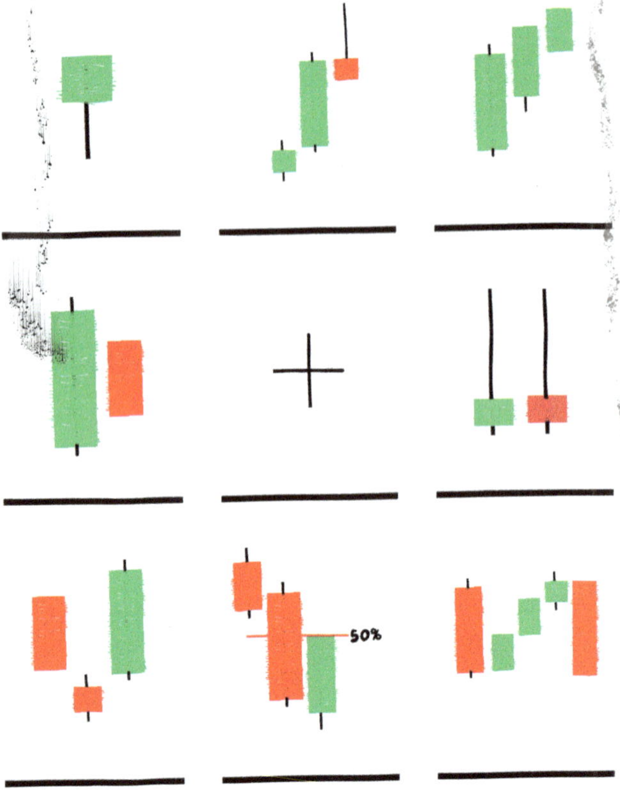

CANDLE KNOWLEDGE

DRAW THE PATTERN

FEEL FREE TO DRAW OUTLINES.

DOUBLE TOP

BEAR FLAG

FALLING WEDGE

RISING WEDGE

TRIPLE TOP

BULL PENNANT

DOUBLE BOTTOM

FALLING WEDGE

BULL FLAG

BOOK'S

CLOSING

6 KEY REMINDERS FOR TRADING CANDLESTICK PATTERNS

When incorporating candlestick patterns into your trading strategy, it's crucial to move beyond simple memorization of formations. For more effective and informed trading decisions, keep these six essential principles in mind:

1. Context is King: Analyze the Bigger Picture

A candlestick pattern's reliability is heavily dependent on the market context in which it appears. A bullish engulfing pattern, for instance, is far more significant at a major support level in an overall uptrend than it is in the middle of a choppy, sideways market. Before acting on any pattern, always consider the prevailing trend, support and resistance levels, and the overall market sentiment. A pattern that contradicts the broader trend should be viewed with skepticism.

2. Seek Confirmation: Don't Trade on a Single Signal

Never rely on a candlestick pattern in isolation. A high-probability trade often comes from the convergence of multiple signals. To confirm a pattern's validity, look for corroborating evidence from other technical indicators. This could include a moving average crossover, a bullish or bearish divergence on the Relative Strength Index (RSI), or a signal from the Moving Average Convergence Divergence (MACD). The more confirming factors you have, the stronger your trading setup.

3. Volume is a Vital Clue

Volume provides insight into the conviction behind a price move. A candlestick pattern accompanied by a significant increase in trading volume is generally more reliable than one formed on low volume.

4. Practice Prudent Risk Management

No candlestick pattern is foolproof. There will always be instances where a seemingly perfect setup fails. Therefore, robust risk management is non-negotiable. Before entering any trade based on a candlestick pattern, you must determine your stop-loss level and your target profit. A common practice is to place a stop-loss below the low of a bullish pattern or above the high of a bearish pattern. Adhering to a proper risk-reward ratio is also essential for long-term profitability.

5. Avoid "Pattern Blindness" and Subjectivity

It can be tempting to see familiar patterns everywhere, especially when you're eager to find a trade. This "pattern blindness" can lead to forcing trades on imperfect or ambiguous formations. Stick to clear and well-defined patterns that adhere to their textbook characteristics as closely as possible. If you have to squint or second-guess whether a formation is a true doji or a hammer, it's likely not a strong enough signal to act upon. Patience and discipline are key; wait for the high-quality setups to emerge.

6. Understand the Timeframe's Influence

The significance of a candlestick pattern is directly tied to the chart's timeframe. A pattern that forms on a daily or weekly chart is substantially more powerful and reliable than the same pattern appearing on a 1-minute or 5-minute chart.

Higher timeframes represent a longer, more protracted battle between buyers and sellers, and their outcome reflects a more definitive shift in market sentiment. Lower timeframes are filled with "noise" and fleeting price movements. While they can be useful for fine-tuning entries, the primary trading signals should be taken from higher timeframes. A strong bullish pattern on a daily chart can serve as a guiding thesis for the entire day or even week, whereas a similar pattern on a 5-minute chart might only be relevant for the next 30 minutes. Always give more weight to patterns that align with the story being told on the longer-term charts.

WHERE TO PUT YOUR KNOWLEDGE TO WORK.

Investopedia

TradingView

TOP FAVORITE

Webull

moomoo

You could try them all, and use it as a sandbox to apply what you're learning from this book!

Trying them all out allows you to see which one you like best.

JULYTHIRTY CO.

by Chaymeriyia Moncrief

HOPE YOU LEARNED A THING...OR 50.